A PLANNER
FOR THE WELL-EDUCATED HEART

_____
School Year

GROWING STRONG ROOT SYSTEMS IN THE HEART

16. 'The Beginning' of Learning
15. Classic Lit., i.e., The Great Books
14. Threads: Art, Music, Architecture, Religion, Science
13. Moral Heroes
12. Stories of Nations
11. History like Landmarks, Signature Biographies, etc.
10. Historical Fiction
9. Short Picturesque Stories
8. Epic and Legendary Heroes, i.e., King Arthur

HEROIC

7. Famous Childhoods, child life in far away lands
6. Children's Classics, i.e., The Secret Garden, A Little Princess
5. Fairy Tales, Mythology

IMAGINATIVE

4. Transitional Stories – part familiar, part imaginative, i.e., Raggedy Ann
3. Short Repetitive Stories, i.e., The Three Bears, also family/nature
2. Picture Books
1. Mother Goose
0. Lullabies

FAMILIAR

"In order to read the 'great' books of Plato, Aristotle, St. Augustine and St. Thomas, we need to replenish the cultural soul that has been depleted and create a place where these works can thrive by cultivating an imaginative ground saturated with fable, fairy tale, stories, rhymes and adventures — the thousand books of Grimm, Andersen, Dickens, Scott, Dumas and the rest. The one thing a great books education will not do is create a moral imagination where there is none."

— John Senior

YEARLY ROTATION PLAN

MONTH 1	MONTH 2	MONTH 3	MONTH 4
1500s: Exploration	1600s: Colonies	1700s: Independence	George Washington
China/Asia India Scandinavia South Seas	Netherlands Spain Spanish Main/Pirates	England Scotland/Ireland/Wales	Greece Rome Italy
Stars	Ocean	Rocks	Plants/Trees
A Mother's Influence	Nature Study	Music	Art

MONTH 5	MONTH 6	MONTH 7	MONTH 8
American Revolution	A New Nation	1800s: Expansion	Abraham Lincoln African Americans/Slavery
France Switzerland Canada	Holy Land Ancient Civilizations	Arabia/Islam/Crusades	Africa Ancient Egypt
Gardening	Insects	Birds	Animals
Poetry	Storytelling	Imagination	History

MONTH 9	MONTH 10	MONTH 11	MONTH 12
Civil War	World Wars	American: Overview	American Biographies
Latin America	Germany Russia Eastern Europe	World: Overview	World Biographies
Human Body			
Writing	Math	Science	Joy

KEY

American History
World History
Nature
Mother's University

Notes

Notes

Notes

MONTH

American History:
World History:
Nature:
Mother's University:

BOOKS / AUDIOS

ENRICHMENT

TO DO
Print. Read. Prepare.

SUPPLIES

FOOD INGREDIENTS

MISCELLANEOUS

MONTH AT-A-GLANCE

MON	TUE	WED	THU	FRI	SAT / SUN

Notes:

WEEK 1

M Music A Art P Poetry S Stories N Nature

MONDAY M A P S N

TUESDAY M A P S N

WEDNESDAY M A P S N

THURSDAY M A P S N

FRIDAY M A P S N

SATURDAY | **SUNDAY**

Notes:

WEEK 2

MONDAY — M A P S N

TUESDAY — M A P S N

WEDNESDAY — M A P S N

THURSDAY — M A P S N

FRIDAY — M A P S N

SATURDAY	SUNDAY

Notes:

WEEK 3

MONDAY — M A P S N

TUESDAY — M A P S N

WEDNESDAY — M A P S N

THURSDAY — M A P S N

FRIDAY — M A P S N

SATURDAY

SUNDAY

Notes:

WEEK 4

MONDAY — M A P S N

TUESDAY — M A P S N

WEDNESDAY — M A P S N

THURSDAY — M A P S N

FRIDAY — M A P S N

SATURDAY

SUNDAY

Notes:

WEEK 5

MONDAY   (M) (A) (P) (S) (N)

TUESDAY   (M) (A) (P) (S) (N)

WEDNESDAY   (M) (A) (P) (S) (N)

THURSDAY   (M) (A) (P) (S) (N)

FRIDAY   (M) (A) (P) (S) (N)

SATURDAY	SUNDAY

MONTH

February

American History: _____
World History: _____
Nature: _____
Mother's University: _____

BOOKS / AUDIOS

ENRICHMENT

TO DO
Print. Read. Prepare.

SUPPLIES

FOOD INGREDIENTS

MISCELLANEOUS

MONTH AT-A-GLANCE

MON	TUE	WED	THU	FRI	SAT / SUN

Notes:

WEEK 1

M Music A Art P Poetry S Stories N Nature

MONDAY — (M) (A) (P) (S) (N)

TUESDAY — (M) (A) (P) (S) (N)

WEDNESDAY — (M) (A) (P) (S) (N)

THURSDAY — (M) (A) (P) (S) (N)

FRIDAY — (M) (A) (P) (S) (N)

SATURDAY | SUNDAY

Notes:

WEEK 2

MONDAY　　　　　　　　　　　　　　　　　　　　　　　　Ⓜ Ⓐ Ⓟ Ⓢ Ⓝ

TUESDAY　　　　　　　　　　　　　　　　　　　　　　　　Ⓜ Ⓐ Ⓟ Ⓢ Ⓝ

WEDNESDAY　　　　　　　　　　　　　　　　　　　　　　Ⓜ Ⓐ Ⓟ Ⓢ Ⓝ

THURSDAY　　　　　　　　　　　　　　　　　　　　　　　Ⓜ Ⓐ Ⓟ Ⓢ Ⓝ

FRIDAY　　　　　　　　　　　　　　　　　　　　　　　　　Ⓜ Ⓐ Ⓟ Ⓢ Ⓝ

SATURDAY | SUNDAY

Notes:

WEEK 3

MONDAY — M A P S N

TUESDAY — M A P S N

WEDNESDAY — M A P S N

THURSDAY — M A P S N

FRIDAY — M A P S N

SATURDAY

SUNDAY

Notes:

WEEK 4

MONDAY M A P S N

TUESDAY M A P S N

WEDNESDAY M A P S N

THURSDAY M A P S N

FRIDAY M A P S N

SATURDAY

SUNDAY

Notes:

WEEK 5

MONDAY — M A P S N

TUESDAY — M A P S N

WEDNESDAY — M A P S N

THURSDAY — M A P S N

FRIDAY — M A P S N

SATURDAY

SUNDAY

MONTH

March

American History: _____
World History: Ireland
Nature: Eggs/birds
Mother's University: _____

BOOKS / AUDIOS

- Geology
- Ireland Map
- Pinterest: Irish Music
- Art

ENRICHMENT

TO DO
Print. Read. Prepare.

- Lent / Easter
- St. Patrick
- Mother's Study

SUPPLIES

FOOD INGREDIENTS

MISCELLANEOUS

MONTH AT-A-GLANCE

MON	TUE	WED	THU	FRI	SAT / SUN

Notes:

WEEK 1

M Music A Art P Poetry S Stories N Nature

MONDAY M A P S N

TUESDAY M A P S N

WEDNESDAY M A P S N

THURSDAY M A P S N

FRIDAY M A P S N

SATURDAY

SUNDAY

Notes:

WEEK 2

MONDAY   Ⓜ Ⓐ Ⓟ Ⓢ Ⓝ

TUESDAY   Ⓜ Ⓐ Ⓟ Ⓢ Ⓝ

WEDNESDAY   Ⓜ Ⓐ Ⓟ Ⓢ Ⓝ

THURSDAY   Ⓜ Ⓐ Ⓟ Ⓢ Ⓝ

FRIDAY   Ⓜ Ⓐ Ⓟ Ⓢ Ⓝ

SATURDAY | **SUNDAY**

Notes:

WEEK 3

MONDAY Ⓜ Ⓐ Ⓟ Ⓢ Ⓝ

TUESDAY Ⓜ Ⓐ Ⓟ Ⓢ Ⓝ

WEDNESDAY Ⓜ Ⓐ Ⓟ Ⓢ Ⓝ

THURSDAY Ⓜ Ⓐ Ⓟ Ⓢ Ⓝ

FRIDAY Ⓜ Ⓐ Ⓟ Ⓢ Ⓝ

SATURDAY | **SUNDAY**

Notes:

WEEK 4

MONDAY — M A P S N

TUESDAY — M A P S N

WEDNESDAY — M A P S N

THURSDAY — M A P S N

FRIDAY — M A P S N

SATURDAY

SUNDAY

Notes:

WEEK 5

MONDAY — M A P S N

TUESDAY — M A P S N

WEDNESDAY — M A P S N

THURSDAY — M A P S N

FRIDAY — M A P S N

SATURDAY

SUNDAY

MONTH

American History:
World History:
Nature:
Mother's University:

BOOKS / AUDIOS

ENRICHMENT

TO DO
Print. Read. Prepare.

SUPPLIES

FOOD INGREDIENTS

MISCELLANEOUS

MONTH AT-A-GLANCE

MON	TUE	WED	THU	FRI	SAT / SUN

Notes:

Notes:

WEEK 1

M Music A Art P Poetry S Stories N Nature

MONDAY — M A P S N

TUESDAY — M A P S N

WEDNESDAY — M A P S N

THURSDAY — M A P S N

FRIDAY — M A P S N

SATURDAY

SUNDAY

Notes:

WEEK 2

MONDAY M A P S N

TUESDAY M A P S N

WEDNESDAY M A P S N

THURSDAY M A P S N

FRIDAY M A P S N

SATURDAY | **SUNDAY**

Notes:

WEEK 3

MONDAY   M A P S N

TUESDAY   M A P S N

WEDNESDAY   M A P S N

THURSDAY   M A P S N

FRIDAY   M A P S N

SATURDAY | SUNDAY

Notes:

WEEK 4

MONDAY M A P S N

TUESDAY M A P S N

WEDNESDAY M A P S N

THURSDAY M A P S N

FRIDAY M A P S N

SATURDAY

SUNDAY

Notes:

Notes:

WEEK 5

MONDAY   M A P S N

TUESDAY   M A P S N

WEDNESDAY   M A P S N

THURSDAY   M A P S N

FRIDAY   M A P S N

SATURDAY	SUNDAY

MONTH

American History:
World History:
Nature:
Mother's University:

BOOKS / AUDIOS

ENRICHMENT

TO DO
Print. Read. Prepare.

SUPPLIES

FOOD INGREDIENTS

MISCELLANEOUS

MONTH AT-A-GLANCE

MON	TUE	WED	THU	FRI	SAT / SUN

Notes:

WEEK 1

M Music A Art P Poetry S Stories N Nature

MONDAY M A P S N

TUESDAY M A P S N

WEDNESDAY M A P S N

THURSDAY M A P S N

FRIDAY M A P S N

SATURDAY

SUNDAY

Notes:

WEEK 2

MONDAY   M A P S N

TUESDAY   M A P S N

WEDNESDAY   M A P S N

THURSDAY   M A P S N

FRIDAY   M A P S N

SATURDAY | **SUNDAY**

Notes:

WEEK 3

MONDAY — M A P S N

TUESDAY — M A P S N

WEDNESDAY — M A P S N

THURSDAY — M A P S N

FRIDAY — M A P S N

SATURDAY

SUNDAY

Notes:

WEEK 4

MONDAY Ⓜ Ⓐ Ⓟ Ⓢ Ⓝ

TUESDAY Ⓜ Ⓐ Ⓟ Ⓢ Ⓝ

WEDNESDAY Ⓜ Ⓐ Ⓟ Ⓢ Ⓝ

THURSDAY Ⓜ Ⓐ Ⓟ Ⓢ Ⓝ

FRIDAY Ⓜ Ⓐ Ⓟ Ⓢ Ⓝ

SATURDAY | **SUNDAY**

Notes:

WEEK 5

MONDAY — M A P S N

TUESDAY — M A P S N

WEDNESDAY — M A P S N

THURSDAY — M A P S N

FRIDAY — M A P S N

SATURDAY

SUNDAY

MONTH

American History: _____
World History: _____
Nature: _____
Mother's University: _____

BOOKS / AUDIOS

ENRICHMENT

TO DO
Print. Read. Prepare.

SUPPLIES

FOOD INGREDIENTS

MISCELLANEOUS

MONTH AT-A-GLANCE

MON	TUE	WED	THU	FRI	SAT / SUN

Notes:

WEEK 1

M Music   A Art   P Poetry   S Stories   N Nature

MONDAY   M A P S N

TUESDAY   M A P S N

WEDNESDAY   M A P S N

THURSDAY   M A P S N

FRIDAY   M A P S N

SATURDAY | SUNDAY

Notes:

WEEK 2

MONDAY M A P S N

TUESDAY M A P S N

WEDNESDAY M A P S N

THURSDAY M A P S N

FRIDAY M A P S N

SATURDAY

SUNDAY

Notes:

WEEK 3

MONDAY (M) (A) (P) (S) (N)

TUESDAY (M) (A) (P) (S) (N)

WEDNESDAY (M) (A) (P) (S) (N)

THURSDAY (M) (A) (P) (S) (N)

FRIDAY (M) (A) (P) (S) (N)

SATURDAY | SUNDAY

Notes:

WEEK 4

MONDAY — M A P S N

TUESDAY — M A P S N

WEDNESDAY — M A P S N

THURSDAY — M A P S N

FRIDAY — M A P S N

SATURDAY

SUNDAY

Notes:

WEEK 5

MONDAY M A P S N

TUESDAY M A P S N

WEDNESDAY M A P S N

THURSDAY M A P S N

FRIDAY M A P S N

SATURDAY

SUNDAY

MONTH

American History:
World History:
Nature:
Mother's University:

BOOKS / AUDIOS

ENRICHMENT

TO DO
Print. Read. Prepare.

SUPPLIES

FOOD INGREDIENTS

MISCELLANEOUS

MONTH AT-A-GLANCE

MON	TUE	WED	THU	FRI	SAT / SUN

Notes:

WEEK 1

M Music A Art P Poetry S Stories N Nature

MONDAY M A P S N

TUESDAY M A P S N

WEDNESDAY M A P S N

THURSDAY M A P S N

FRIDAY M A P S N

SATURDAY

SUNDAY

Notes:

WEEK 2

MONDAY   (M) (A) (P) (S) (N)

TUESDAY   (M) (A) (P) (S) (N)

WEDNESDAY   (M) (A) (P) (S) (N)

THURSDAY   (M) (A) (P) (S) (N)

FRIDAY   (M) (A) (P) (S) (N)

SATURDAY | **SUNDAY**

Notes:

WEEK 3

MONDAY — M A P S N

TUESDAY — M A P S N

WEDNESDAY — M A P S N

THURSDAY — M A P S N

FRIDAY — M A P S N

SATURDAY

SUNDAY

Notes:

WEEK 4

MONDAY — M A P S N

TUESDAY — M A P S N

WEDNESDAY — M A P S N

THURSDAY — M A P S N

FRIDAY — M A P S N

SATURDAY

SUNDAY

Notes:

WEEK 5

MONDAY — M A P S N

TUESDAY — M A P S N

WEDNESDAY — M A P S N

THURSDAY — M A P S N

FRIDAY — M A P S N

SATURDAY | **SUNDAY**

MONTH

American History:
World History:
Nature:
Mother's University:

BOOKS / AUDIOS

ENRICHMENT

TO DO
Print. Read. Prepare.

SUPPLIES

FOOD INGREDIENTS

MISCELLANEOUS

MONTH AT-A-GLANCE

MON	TUE	WED	THU	FRI	SAT / SUN

Notes:

WEEK 1

M Music A Art P Poetry S Stories N Nature

MONDAY — M A P S N

TUESDAY — M A P S N

WEDNESDAY — M A P S N

THURSDAY — M A P S N

FRIDAY — M A P S N

SATURDAY

SUNDAY

Notes:

WEEK 2

MONDAY Ⓜ Ⓐ Ⓟ Ⓢ Ⓝ

TUESDAY Ⓜ Ⓐ Ⓟ Ⓢ Ⓝ

WEDNESDAY Ⓜ Ⓐ Ⓟ Ⓢ Ⓝ

THURSDAY Ⓜ Ⓐ Ⓟ Ⓢ Ⓝ

FRIDAY Ⓜ Ⓐ Ⓟ Ⓢ Ⓝ

SATURDAY | **SUNDAY**

Notes:

WEEK 3

MONDAY — M A P S N

TUESDAY — M A P S N

WEDNESDAY — M A P S N

THURSDAY — M A P S N

FRIDAY — M A P S N

SATURDAY | **SUNDAY**

Notes:

WEEK 4

MONDAY — M A P S N

TUESDAY — M A P S N

WEDNESDAY — M A P S N

THURSDAY — M A P S N

FRIDAY — M A P S N

SATURDAY | **SUNDAY**

Notes:

WEEK 5

MONDAY — M A P S N

TUESDAY — M A P S N

WEDNESDAY — M A P S N

THURSDAY — M A P S N

FRIDAY — M A P S N

SATURDAY

SUNDAY

MONTH

American History: _____
World History: _____
Nature: _____
Mother's University: _____

BOOKS / AUDIOS

ENRICHMENT

TO DO
Print. Read. Prepare.

SUPPLIES

FOOD INGREDIENTS

MISCELLANEOUS

MONTH AT-A-GLANCE

MON	TUE	WED	THU	FRI	SAT / SUN

Notes:

WEEK 1

M Music A Art P Poetry S Stories N Nature

| MONDAY | M A P S N |

| TUESDAY | M A P S N |

| WEDNESDAY | M A P S N |

| THURSDAY | M A P S N |

| FRIDAY | M A P S N |

| SATURDAY | SUNDAY |

Notes:

WEEK 2

MONDAY · M A P S N

TUESDAY · M A P S N

WEDNESDAY · M A P S N

THURSDAY · M A P S N

FRIDAY · M A P S N

SATURDAY | SUNDAY

Notes:

WEEK 3

MONDAY M A P S N

TUESDAY M A P S N

WEDNESDAY M A P S N

THURSDAY M A P S N

FRIDAY M A P S N

SATURDAY | SUNDAY

Notes:

WEEK 4

MONDAY Ⓜ Ⓐ Ⓟ Ⓢ Ⓝ

TUESDAY Ⓜ Ⓐ Ⓟ Ⓢ Ⓝ

WEDNESDAY Ⓜ Ⓐ Ⓟ Ⓢ Ⓝ

THURSDAY Ⓜ Ⓐ Ⓟ Ⓢ Ⓝ

FRIDAY Ⓜ Ⓐ Ⓟ Ⓢ Ⓝ

SATURDAY | **SUNDAY**

Notes:

WEEK 5

MONDAY M A P S N

TUESDAY M A P S N

WEDNESDAY M A P S N

THURSDAY M A P S N

FRIDAY M A P S N

SATURDAY | SUNDAY

MONTH

American History:
World History:
Nature:
Mother's University:

BOOKS / AUDIOS

ENRICHMENT

TO DO
Print. Read. Prepare.

SUPPLIES

FOOD INGREDIENTS

MISCELLANEOUS

MONTH AT-A-GLANCE

MON	TUE	WED	THU	FRI	SAT / SUN

Notes:

WEEK 1

M Music A Art P Poetry S Stories N Nature

MONDAY
Ⓜ Ⓐ Ⓟ Ⓢ Ⓝ

TUESDAY
Ⓜ Ⓐ Ⓟ Ⓢ Ⓝ

WEDNESDAY
Ⓜ Ⓐ Ⓟ Ⓢ Ⓝ

THURSDAY
Ⓜ Ⓐ Ⓟ Ⓢ Ⓝ

FRIDAY
Ⓜ Ⓐ Ⓟ Ⓢ Ⓝ

SATURDAY

SUNDAY

Notes:

WEEK 2

MONDAY   Ⓜ Ⓐ Ⓟ Ⓢ Ⓝ

TUESDAY   Ⓜ Ⓐ Ⓟ Ⓢ Ⓝ

WEDNESDAY   Ⓜ Ⓐ Ⓟ Ⓢ Ⓝ

THURSDAY   Ⓜ Ⓐ Ⓟ Ⓢ Ⓝ

FRIDAY   Ⓜ Ⓐ Ⓟ Ⓢ Ⓝ

SATURDAY | **SUNDAY**

Notes:

WEEK 3

MONDAY   (M) (A) (P) (S) (N)

TUESDAY   (M) (A) (P) (S) (N)

WEDNESDAY   (M) (A) (P) (S) (N)

THURSDAY   (M) (A) (P) (S) (N)

FRIDAY   (M) (A) (P) (S) (N)

SATURDAY | **SUNDAY**

Notes:

WEEK 4

MONDAY M A P S N

TUESDAY M A P S N

WEDNESDAY M A P S N

THURSDAY M A P S N

FRIDAY M A P S N

SATURDAY | SUNDAY

Notes:

WEEK 5

MONDAY M A P S N

TUESDAY M A P S N

WEDNESDAY M A P S N

THURSDAY M A P S N

FRIDAY M A P S N

SATURDAY | SUNDAY

MONTH

American History: _____
World History: _____
Nature: _____
Mother's University: _____

BOOKS / AUDIOS

ENRICHMENT

TO DO
Print. Read. Prepare.

SUPPLIES

FOOD INGREDIENTS

MISCELLANEOUS

MONTH AT-A-GLANCE

MON	TUE	WED	THU	FRI	SAT / SUN

Notes:

WEEK 1

M Music A Art P Poetry S Stories N Nature

MONDAY — M A P S N

TUESDAY — M A P S N

WEDNESDAY — M A P S N

THURSDAY — M A P S N

FRIDAY — M A P S N

SATURDAY

SUNDAY

Notes:

WEEK 2

MONDAY — M A P S N

TUESDAY — M A P S N

WEDNESDAY — M A P S N

THURSDAY — M A P S N

FRIDAY — M A P S N

SATURDAY | **SUNDAY**

Notes:

WEEK 3

MONDAY — M A P S N

TUESDAY — M A P S N

WEDNESDAY — M A P S N

THURSDAY — M A P S N

FRIDAY — M A P S N

SATURDAY

SUNDAY

Notes:

WEEK 4

MONDAY M A P S N

TUESDAY M A P S N

WEDNESDAY M A P S N

THURSDAY M A P S N

FRIDAY M A P S N

SATURDAY

SUNDAY

Notes:

WEEK 5

MONDAY — M A P S N

TUESDAY — M A P S N

WEDNESDAY — M A P S N

THURSDAY — M A P S N

FRIDAY — M A P S N

SATURDAY | SUNDAY

MONTH

American History:
World History:
Nature:
Mother's University:

BOOKS / AUDIOS

ENRICHMENT

TO DO
Print. Read. Prepare.

SUPPLIES

FOOD INGREDIENTS

MISCELLANEOUS

MONTH AT-A-GLANCE

MON	TUE	WED	THU	FRI	SAT / SUN

Notes:

WEEK 1

M Music A Art P Poetry S Stories N Nature

MONDAY — M A P S N

TUESDAY — M A P S N

WEDNESDAY — M A P S N

THURSDAY — M A P S N

FRIDAY — M A P S N

SATURDAY

SUNDAY

Notes:

WEEK 2

MONDAY   Ⓜ Ⓐ Ⓟ Ⓢ Ⓝ

TUESDAY   Ⓜ Ⓐ Ⓟ Ⓢ Ⓝ

WEDNESDAY   Ⓜ Ⓐ Ⓟ Ⓢ Ⓝ

THURSDAY   Ⓜ Ⓐ Ⓟ Ⓢ Ⓝ

FRIDAY   Ⓜ Ⓐ Ⓟ Ⓢ Ⓝ

SATURDAY | **SUNDAY**

Notes:

WEEK 3

MONDAY — M A P S N

TUESDAY — M A P S N

WEDNESDAY — M A P S N

THURSDAY — M A P S N

FRIDAY — M A P S N

SATURDAY

SUNDAY

Notes:

WEEK 4

MONDAY   M A P S N

TUESDAY   M A P S N

WEDNESDAY   M A P S N

THURSDAY   M A P S N

FRIDAY   M A P S N

SATURDAY

SUNDAY

Notes:

WEEK 5

MONDAY | M A P S N

TUESDAY | M A P S N

WEDNESDAY | M A P S N

THURSDAY | M A P S N

FRIDAY | M A P S N

SATURDAY | SUNDAY

A MOTHER'S INFLUENCE

Mother's University

NATURE STUDY

Mother's University

MUSIC

Mother's University

ART

Mother's University

POETRY

Mother's University

STORYTELLING

Mother's University

IMAGINATION

Mother's University

HISTORY

Mother's University

WRITING

Mother's University

MATH

Mother's University

SCIENCE

Mother's University

Mother's University

CONTACTS

Name:
Phone:
E-mail:
Address:
    Street and No.   Apt. No.   City   State   Zip Code

Notes:

Name:
Phone:
E-mail:
Address:
    Street and No.   Apt. No.   City   State   Zip Code

Notes:

Name:
Phone:
E-mail:
Address:
    Street and No.   Apt. No.   City   State   Zip Code

Notes:

Name:
Phone:
E-mail:
Address:
    Street and No.   Apt. No.   City   State   Zip Code

Notes:

Name:
Phone:
E-mail:
Address:
    Street and No.   Apt. No.   City   State   Zip Code

Notes:

Name:
Phone:
E-mail:
Address:
    Street and No.   Apt. No.   City   State   Zip Code

Notes:

Name:
Phone:
E-mail:
Address:
    Street and No.   Apt. No.   City   State   Zip Code

Notes:

CONTACTS

Name:
Phone:
E-mail:
Address:
Street and No.   Apt. No.   City   State   Zip Code

Notes:

Name:
Phone:
E-mail:
Address:
Street and No.   Apt. No.   City   State   Zip Code

Notes:

Name:
Phone:
E-mail:
Address:
Street and No.   Apt. No.   City   State   Zip Code

Notes:

Name:
Phone:
E-mail:
Address:
Street and No.   Apt. No.   City   State   Zip Code

Notes:

Name:
Phone:
E-mail:
Address:
Street and No.   Apt. No.   City   State   Zip Code

Notes:

Name:
Phone:
E-mail:
Address:
Street and No.   Apt. No.   City   State   Zip Code

Notes:

Name:
Phone:
E-mail:
Address:
Street and No.   Apt. No.   City   State   Zip Code

Notes:

THE SONG IS NEVER ENDED
FROM "MY GARDEN OF MEMORIES" BY KATE DOUGLAS WIGGIN

In childhood, whenever I read Hans Christian Andersen's fairy-tales—which was all too seldom, for we had but one copy of the book—I always turned first to the story of the Flax; and as my sister and I grew older and were incessantly telling or reading stories to children, it exerted a great satisfaction, indeed a great influence, over me. It seemed a little piece of religion, and in some way a philosophy of life.

Do you remember how the Flax said to itself one fine summer morning?—"I am strong and tall. I am in full bloom; and every day something delightful happens to me. Oh! This is a beautiful world!"

A Hedge-Stake, near by, you know, overheard the Flax and grumbled: "It takes those who have knots in their stems to know the world!"—and he creaked out a mournful song:

"Snip, snap, snurre,
Basse lurre:
The song is ended!"

"Oh, no!" cried the Flax; "the song is not ended, it is hardly begun. Every day the sunshine gladdens, or the rain refreshes me. I know that I am growing. I know that I am in full blossom. I am the happiest of all creatures."

I used to feel even then that the Hedge-Stake was wrong in his philosophy of existence; but very soon in the story the Flax, now full-grown, was pulled up by the roots, laid in water till it was almost drowned, and set by the fire until it was almost roasted.

"One must not complain," said the Flax. "If I've suffered something, I'm being made into something." And when it was put upon the wheel and spun into thread, and the thread woven into a web, still it sang its song of content as the wheel whirred and the shuttle shot to and fro. (I think two little girls, sitting by an open fire, with a few tears falling on the page of the beloved book, learned something just then—not through the head, but the heart!)

Then the Flax was spread upon the grass as a long piece of white linen, the finest in the parish, and there were many changes after that—snipping and cutting and making into garments—and the Flax said: "See how little the Hedge-Stake knew when he told me the song was ended; look what I have become! This was my destiny. Now I shall be of some use in the world. I am the happiest of all creatures."

At last the garments were worn quite to rags; and then they were cut into smaller bits and softened and boiled till they became white paper.

"What a glorious surprise!" cried the Flax. "Now perhaps a poet may come and write his thoughts upon me. See how I am led on from glory to glory—I who was only a little blue flower growing in the fields. Ah! The poor Hedge-Stake, how little he knew about life!"

And truly a poet did come and write beautiful thoughts on the shining white leaves, and they were sent to the printers and made into books.

"This is best of all!" said the Flax. "Now I shall sit at home, like an honored grandfather, and my books will travel over all lands. How happy I am! Each time I think the song is ended, it begins again in a more beautiful way!"

But now the paper was thrust into a barrel and sold to a grocer for wrapping his butter and sugar.

"I had not thought of this!" said the Flax (though the two little girls had, and a hundred readings could not prevent momentary tears). "But, after all, it is better, for I have been so hurried from one stage of my life to another that I have never had time to think! After work, it is well to rest. Now I can reflect on my real condition."

But it did not happen as the Flax had thought, for the grocer's children were fond of burning paper on the hearth. They liked the flash of the flames up the chimney, the gray ashes below and the red sparks careering here and there, and they often danced and sang when the fire was flashing its brightest; so they pulled all the paper from the barrel one day and set it afire.

Whis-sh! went the blaze up the chimney. It soared higher than the Flax had ever lifted its blue flowers, and glistened as the white linen had never glistened.

"Now I'm mounting straight up to the sun!" cried a voice far above the chimney, and, more delicate than the flames, invisible to human eyes, a myriad tiny beings floated in the air above, many, many more than there had been blossoms on the Flax.

Down below, the children sang the rhyme of the Hedge-Stake over the dead ashes:

"Snip, snap, snurre,
Basse lurre;
The song is ended!"

But the little invisible beings in the air above them sang together, as clearly as if there had been a thousand voices in unison: "The song is never ended; the most beautiful is yet to come; we know it, and therefore we are the happiest of all!"